Psalms for
Mothers

Presented to:

_____

Presented by:

_____

Date:

_____

Psalms for Mothers

God's Gift

of Endless Love,

Joy, and Encouragement

Honor Books
Tulsa, Oklahoma

Psalms for Mothers
ISBN 1-56292-844-9

Copyright © 2001 by GRQ Ink, Inc.
1948 Green Hills Blvd.
Franklin, Tennessee 37067

Published by Honor Books
P. O. Box 55388
Tulsa, Oklahoma 74155

Developed by GRQ Ink, Inc.
Manuscript written by Faith Billings
Cover and text design by Whisner Design Group
Composition by Educational Publishing Concepts, Inc.

By You I have been upheld from birth;
You are He who took me out of
my mother's womb.
My praise shall
be continually of You.

PSALM 71:6 NKJV

God Loves a Mother's Prayer

His delight is in the law of the LORD,
and on his law he meditates day and night.
He is like a tree planted by streams of water,
which yields its fruit in season
and whose leaf does not wither.

PSALM 1:2-3 NIV

Mothers are great prayer-makers. One look at our children as they leave for school, play with their friends in the front yard, or open birthday presents can bring a prayer to our lips. We pray constantly for their protection. We happily give thanks for their joy. We beg God to guide them as they grow. We are always

asking God to help us be good mothers. God loves a mother's prayers. We talk so much with God because our children are so precious. There's so much to say—we want our children to be held in the palm of God's hand.

God has so much to say to us when we listen with our hearts. God tells us to have faith in His goodness, to not worry. God tells us that He loves our children even more than we do. God promises to work through us as we raise our children the best we can.

We can pray to God today because God listens to our prayers.

I cried unto the LORD with my voice,
and he heard me out of his holy hill.

PSALM 3:4 KJV

In the morning, O LORD, You will hear my voice;
In the morning I will order my prayer to You
and eagerly watch.

PSALM 5:3 NASB

God Is Our Shield

You, O Lord, are a shield around me,
my glory, and the one who lifts up my head.

PSALM 3:3 NRSV

Mothers have a special job—to protect our children so that they can grow up healthy and happy. We make sure they eat a balanced diet and brush their teeth. We take them to the doctor for regular checkups. We hold their hands when we cross the street. We make sure they wear their raincoats in the rain.

We also call on God to protect our children, to shield them with the brightness of His light, to hide them in the shadow of His wings. Praying for God's protection is as important as making sure our kids have their seat belts fastened. God covers our children with His goodness and mercy. God journeys with them by day and watches over them by night.

God is our shield too. God watches over mothers and helps us to raise healthy, happy children. God's shield is very big—it covers us and our children as surely as a warm, downy blanket on a cold winter's night.

We can relax today knowing that God is our shield.

God's my island hideaway,
keeps danger far from the shore,
throws garlands of hosannas around my neck.

PSALM 32:7 THE MESSAGE

You bless righteous people, O LORD.
Like a large shield, you surround them with your favor.

PSALM 5:12 GOD'S WORD

Love Watches Over Us

*I sleep and wake up refreshed
because you, LORD, protect me.*

PSALM 3:5 CEV

જી

It's been another busy day. Carpool in the morning. A soccer match and a swim meet in the afternoon. Then there was dinner to cook and homework to supervise. Through all the activity God's love watches over our kids and us moms.

Because God's love watches over us, we can go about the business of raising our children free from worry or anxiety. No matter how busy we are, God's love, like the air we breathe, sustains us. God's love wraps about us, like a comfy, well-worn sweater. No matter what we do, we can count on the power of God's love watching over us to make everything all right. No matter where we go, the love of God follows us and gives us the strength we need to be good moms.

God's first words to us in the morning are *I love you*, and God's last words to us at night are *I love you*. With love like that, we can do anything.

જી

The power of God's love is with us now.

I trust in your love.
My heart is happy because you saved me.

PSALM 13:5 NCV

The LORD is merciful, compassionate, patient,
and always ready to forgive.

PSALM 145:8 GOD'S WORD

Morning with God

But I will sing of your might;
I will sing aloud of your steadfast love in the morning.
For you have been a fortress for me
and a refuge in the day of my distress.

PSALM 59:16 NRSV

*M*ornings are not necessarily the most peaceful time of the day, especially on school days. We have to get the kids out of bed and into clothes. Get a little breakfast into them and supervise teeth brushing. Lunches are packed and distributed. Finally, the kids are off to school—and then it's our turn to get ready to go to work.

Thank God for weekends! We can get up a little early on a Saturday before the whole house wakes up, make a cup of tea, wrap up in a throw on the couch, and have a good talk with God. Saturday mornings are a good time to ask God for what we need. We spend the rest of the week making sure our families have what they need. Now it's our turn. When we sit quietly on the couch and listen carefully, our hearts will tell us what we need from God.

*G*od listens carefully to hear what it is we want from Him.

O LORD, You have heard the desire of the humble;
You will strengthen their heart, you will incline Your ear.

PSALM 10:17 NASB

O pen up before GOD, keep nothing back;
he'll do whatever needs to be done.

PSALM 37:5 THE MESSAGE

The Wonder of God

Here I am, your invited guest —
it's incredible!
I enter your house; here I am,
prostrate in your inner sanctum.

PSALM 5:7 THE MESSAGE

✧

Every mother has experienced the power of wonder. When we first saw our babies, we were overwhelmed by wonder. As our children were laid in our arms for the first time, the wonder and awe of this complete and perfect little child dissolved us to tears of joy to see what God had created.

Our children may be babies now, or be teenagers, or have families of their own, but mothers can still experience the wonder of God. Whenever we look carefully at our children, whether they're tiny-tots or grown-ups, we can see God's handiwork in them. When we see how God is at work in their lives, we are overwhelmed with wonder at the goodness of God. It is not unlike the first time we held them close and were filled with wonder and joy to see what God had created.

✧

We can look carefully at our children
and know the wonder of God.

There will be an abundance
of grain in the earth,
On the top of the mountains;
Its fruit shall wave like Lebanon;
And those of the city
shall flourish like grass of the earth.

Psalm 72:16 nkjv

From everlasting to everlasting,
the Lord's mercy is on those who fear him.
His righteousness belongs
to their children and grandchildren.

Psalm 103:17 god's word

A Reason to Rejoice

Let all who take refuge in You be glad,
Let them ever sing for joy;
And may You shelter them,
That those who love Your name may exult in You.

PSALM 5:11 NASB

Mothers whose bedroom has ever been invaded by frightened kids on a stormy, thundering night know that her children look to her to keep them safe. Our children look to us to keep them safe from scary things—thunder and lightning, monsters under the bed, and things that go bump in the night. We hold them close and chase the monsters away and tell them there's nothing to be afraid of. We're moms. It's our job.

It's God's job to take care of mothers. We can run to God anytime and be held in His loving arms. We can trust God to chase away all the worries and concerns we naturally have for our children. We can listen in the quiet of the night to hear God telling us there's nothing to be afraid of. Our God loves us, cares for us, and protects us. What a reason to rejoice and be glad!

We can rejoice because it's God's job to take care of us.

They will sing about what the LORD has done,
because the LORD's glory is great.
Though the LORD is supreme,
he takes care of those who are humble,
but he stays away from the proud.

PSALM 138:5-6 NCV

What's more, our hearts brim with joy
since we've taken for our own his holy name.

PSALM 33:21 THE MESSAGE

God's Children

Thou hast made him a little lower than the angels, and hast crowned him with glory and honour.

PSALM 8:5 KJV

Mothers know that underneath the dirt and scruffiness from the playground, and behind the mischievousness and unwillingness to clean their plates at dinner our children seem like angels. When

we see our children peacefully sound asleep, we are convinced that our children do indeed have heavenly origins.

Our children are God's children—and so are we, their mothers. For we, too, are special creatures among all God's creation. We are God's children, loved best and most by God. God has marked us as His own—He has crowned us with honor and glory. Like the angels in heaven, we shine with the love of God, our Father.

Now God has trusted us to raise and love and protect our children. We do with a fierce mother's love that shines brighter and stronger than the noonday sun.

We are bright and shining angels, touched by God's love.

You created my inmost being;
you knit me together in my mother's womb.

Psalm 139:13 NIV

The Lord is good;
his steadfast love endures forever,
and his faithfulness to all generations.

Psalm 100:5 NRSV

Bountiful Gifts

*I will sing unto the LORD, because he hath
dealt bountifully with me.*

PSALM 13:6 KJV

*L*ove is a mother's greatest characteristic, but the next greatest feature a mother has is her unlimited ability to give. Mothers are natural givers. Love inspires all our gifts to our children. Of course, we give our children the basic necessities of life—food, clothing, and shelter; we give them education; we give them medical care. We also give limitless time and attention to help them grow into good and loving adults. We make sure they learn about God and His ways, and how much God loves them.

Just as we give good gifts to our children, God gives good gifts to us. God blesses us every day with faith and courage to raise our children well. God touches us with His mercy and forgiveness so that when we make mistakes, we can try again. God wraps us in His love, which we give freely to our children.

*G*od gives us gifts every moment today.

Praise the LORD, all you nations!
Extol him, all you peoples!
For great is his steadfast love toward us,
and the faithfulness of the LORD endures forever.
Praise the LORD!

PSALM 117:1-2 NRSV

O LORD my God, you have done many miracles for us.
Your plans for us are too numerous to list.
If I tried to recite all your wonderful deeds,
I would never come to the end of them.

PSALM 40:5 NLT

A Mother's Way

LORD, who may abide in Your tabernacle?
Who may dwell in Your holy hill?
He who walks uprightly,
And works righteousness,
And speaks the truth in his heart.

PSALM 15:1-2 NKJV

It's been said that imitation is the highest form of flattery. Children love to imitate their mothers. Whether they are playing

house or mimicking our conversation, children practice at being grown-ups by pretending they are the moms. Children naturally want to follow their mothers wherever they go, whatever they do, and whatever they say. Mothers show their children the way through life.

Part of our job is to show our children how to live so that they can follow us into happy adulthood. We speak truthfully to our children and show them by our actions how much God loves them. This is a mother's way—to "imitate" God's love. When we speak and live God's love, our children naturally want to follow us and be like us. We raise our children to be merciful, wise, and loving grown-ups.

Today we travel a mother's way and show our children
how to follow God's way.

I am constantly aware of your unfailing love,
and I have lived according to your truth.

PSALM 26:3 NLT

LORD, you do everything for me.
LORD your love continues forever.
Do not leave us, whom you made.

PSALM 138:8 NCV

A Mother's Identity

I said to the LORD,
"You are my Lord. Without you, I have nothing good."

PSALM 16:2 GOD'S WORD

❧

Mothers are many things. We are lovers, caregivers, and providers. We are teachers, referees, and drivers. We are organizers, cheerleaders, and champions. We love being all those things because we love being moms.

We have been touched by God's goodness. We have been chosen to be God's special people—mothers. God has planted a special kind of love in our hearts. It is a love without end. It is that love that marks us as God's chosen ones. It is that love we freely share with our children whether today we're cooking short order or driving carpool or supervising homework. We know deep in our hearts how much God loves us.

❧

We are mothers, chosen by God's love.

Because you are my help,
I sing in the shadow of your wings.
My soul clings to you;
your right hand upholds me.

PSALM 63:7-8 NIV

❧

For the sake of the Temple of the LORD,
our God, I wish good for her.

PSALM 122:9 NCV

Our Mothers before Us

The boundary lines have fallen for me in pleasant places;
surely I have a delightful inheritance.

PSALM 16:6 NIV

Motherhood is an ancient path we travel. Our mothers, our grandmothers, and all our great-grandmothers before us have traveled motherhood's way. Our "mother's intuition" is really a quiet knowledge stored up in our hearts, learned from all our mothers gone before us. Motherhood is a "delightful inheritance."

God has given us the heritage of motherhood. We are the heirs of motherly love before us; and we are the stewards of the motherly love that will come after us through our children. We are links in a vast chain of God's own making, passing on from mother to child that which is good and loving and true. As mothers we can be proud and humble at the same time for all we've inherited. We can be grateful to all our female ancestors—our mothers, who've handed us the torch of sacred motherhood.

We stand as a link in a long chain of motherly love,
blessed and held together by God.

A posterity shall serve Him.
It will be recounted of the Lord
to the next generation,
They will come and declare His righteousness
to a people who will be born,
That He has done this.

PSALM 22:30 31 NKJV

Your kingdom will never end, and you will rule forever.
Our LORD, you keep your word
and do everything you say.

PSALM 145:13 CEV

Motherhood's Solid Foundation

I have set the LORD always before me;
Because He is at my right hand
I shall not be moved.

If we pick up any family focused magazine today, we can find countless tips and guides to help us be better mothers. Our world will always be filled with teachers and leaders of various child-rearing techniques and fads. As helpful as some of these guides may be, mothers can always turn to a more solid foundation.

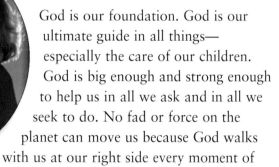

God is our foundation. God is our ultimate guide in all things—especially the care of our children. God is big enough and strong enough to help us in all we ask and in all we seek to do. No fad or force on the planet can move us because God walks with us at our right side every moment of every day. We can turn to God and open our hearts, confident in God's mercy and love. We can place our precious children in God's gentle, loving hands.

Our solid foundation is God,
who holds us in the palm of His hand.

May He send you help from the sanctuary
And support you from Zion!

PSALM 20:2 NASB

He is the one who made heaven and earth,
the sea, and everything in them.
He is the one who keeps every promise forever.

PSALM 146:6 NLT

Enjoying God

You have made known to me the path of life;
you will fill me with joy in your presence,
with eternal pleasures at your right hand.

PSALM 16:11 NIV

A lot of times being a mother is fun. When we play with our children, it's almost like we get to be kids again. We get to play dolls and go to tea parties. Or we get to ride bikes and build pretend forts. Sometimes we get to go to Disneyland.

Play is important to a mother's walk with God too. God enjoys us—and God wants to be enjoyed by us. God wants us to take pleasure in Him. That means we can have fun with God. We don't have to be serious all the time—we can let God into our playtime with our kids; we can lie in a hammock and daydream with God; we can take a long walk with God and not talk about anything much at all. Our relationship with God is to be enjoyed. Today, do something with God just for the fun of it.

Today there's time to enjoy God.

Sing for joy to God our strength;
shout aloud to the God of Jacob!
Begin the music, strike the tambourine,
play the melodious harp and lyre.
Sound the ram's horn at the New Moon,
and when the moon is full, on the day of our Feast.

PSALM 81:1-3 NIV

So that my soul may praise you and not be silent.
O LORD my God, I will give thanks to you forever.

PSALM 30:12 NRSV

A Mother's Prayer

I call upon you, for you will answer me, O God;
incline your ear to me, hear my words.

PSALM 17:6 NRSV

Mothers spend a lot of time listening. When our children are young, we listen to their endless questions about how the world works and why it works the way it does. When our children are teenagers we listen to them as they tell us all about their trials and tribulations at school, and about their new boyfriends or girlfriends. When our children marry and have children of their own, we love to listen to stories about our grandchildren.

God spends a lot of time listening to mothers. God listens to us tell Him how proud we are of our children. God listens to us when we ask for strength and help to be the best mothers we can be. God listens to us as we place our precious children in His loving arms. God loves to listen to a mother's prayers. Know that whenever we call on God, He listens to every word we say.

God loves to listen to a mother's prayers.

Enjoy serving the Lord,
and he will give you what
you want.

Psalm 37:4 NCV

I hope in You, O Lord;
You will answer, O Lord
my God.

Psalm 38:15 NASB

The Love of God

"I love You, O LORD, my strength."
The LORD is my rock and my fortress and my deliverer,
My God, my rock, in whom I take refuge;
My shield and the horn of my salvation, my stronghold.

PSALM 18:1-2 NASB

❧

Everything about motherhood can be summed up in one word—*love*. Everything we do, everything we say, every ounce of our being, is motivated by love. Our giving, our patience, our compassion, our understanding, our hope—all of motherhood's qualities are rooted in the love we have for our children.

Everything about God can also be summed up in one word—*love*. As hard as it is to imagine, God's love for us is deeper, more powerful, and more all-knowing than even a mother's love. There is nothing we can do or think or say that can keep God from loving us. God follows us into the most secret places of our hearts to tell us how much He loves us. We are God's children—and God loves us fiercely, deeply, and eternally.

❧

God's love for us is so great that nothing in heaven or on earth can separate us from Him.

Yea, though I walk through the valley of the shadow of death, I will fear no evil: for thou art with me; thy rod and thy staff they comfort me.

PSALM 23:4 KJV

Pour out your unfailing love on those who love you; give justice to those with honest hearts.

PSALM 36:10 NLT

A Mother's Night-Light

*Thou wilt light my candle: the LORD my God
will enlighten my darkness.*

PSALM 18:28 KJV

"If you turn off the lights, it'll be dark and the monsters in the closet will come out and get me!" What mother hasn't heard, at some time or other, a child's reason like this one for keeping a light on at bedtime? So we compromise—we turn out the main light in the room, but we turn on a night-light to keep the monsters away.

Our faith in God is a mother's "night-light." Unfortunately, we can't see into our children's futures—the way is dark and hidden from our view, but we can hope that our children's futures will be bright because we believe God loves them and holds them in the palm of His hand. It's okay that we can't see into our children's future—because we know God, who is our lamp, is there ahead of us lighting the way.

God makes our children's futures bright.

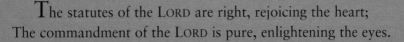

The statutes of the LORD are right, rejoicing the heart;
The commandment of the LORD is pure, enlightening the eyes.

PSALM 19:8 NKJV

You will help me, Lord God, and keep me from falling.

PSALM 54:4 CEV

God's Glory

*The heavens declare the glory of God;
the skies proclaim the work of his hands.*

PSALM 19:1 NIV

"*T*winkle, twinkle little star" is one of the first tunes a child learns to sing. Children seem naturally drawn to the stars; they love to look up at the heavens, their imaginations winging through time and space. Our children are constantly pointing us to the glory of God.

We mothers have a lot to teach our children, but our children have a lot to teach us as well. Maybe children can show us the glory of God in the heavens because they've so recently come from God. Not yet set in adult ways, their minds are still fresh and full of God's glory. On a warm summer's evening, we can let our children take us by the hand and lead us out to the backyard. There we can look up at the soft night sky, full of stars, the handiwork of God—and we can let the children tell us stories of what they see there.

*T*he glory of God shines over us. All we have to do is look up.

The glory of the LORD shall endure for ever: the LORD shall rejoice in his works.

PSALM 104:31 KJV

Who can forget the wonders he performs?
How gracious and merciful is our LORD!
He gives food to those who trust him;
he always remembers his covenant.

PSALM 111:4-5 NLT

A Mother's Powerful Words

Let the words of my mouth and the meditation of my heart
Be acceptable in Your sight,
O LORD, my rock and my Redeemer.

PSALM 19:14 NASB

A mother's words are very powerful. Our words instruct our children, telling them right from wrong. Our words communicate our deep love and caring. Our words correct our children when they've misbehaved. A mother's words have a tremendous impact on the shape of our children's lives and spirits.

Our words are powerful in another way. Our words have a tremendous impact on God. God listens carefully to what we have to say—and He is influenced by what we say too. So we must choose our words carefully. Our prayers to God should always be said with love and honor and wonder— and always end in gratitude for the blessings of this life. We want the words of our mouth to be pleasing and acceptable to God, who loves us and wants to give us His very best.

May the words of our mouths be acceptable to God today.

PRAISE THE LORD!
I will thank the LORD with all my heart
as I meet with his godly people.

PSALM 111:1 NLT

Our Heart's Desire

*May he give you the desire of your heart
and make all your plans succeed.*

PSALM 20:4 NIV

A mother wants the best of everything for her children. We naturally want our kids to have the best homes, the best clothes, and the best schools. We want them to have the brightest futures. We want them to be successful in work and in life. So far as it is within our power, we want to give them the desires of their hearts.

We are God's children. God naturally wants us to have the very best of everything life has to offer. Even more, God longs to give us our hearts' deepest desires. What do our hearts desire the most? If we look long and hard and deeply into the most secret places of our hearts, we find this simple desire—we want God. We want our children to want God more than anything in the world. It is that desire above all others that God is delighted to grant.

May God grant all your desires and fulfill all your plans.

I truly believe
I will live to see the LORD's goodness.

PSALM 27:13 NCV

As for me, I trust in You, O LORD,
I say, "You are my God."

PSALM 31:14 NASB

The Great Shepherd

The LORD is my shepherd; I shall not want.
He makes me to lie down in green pastures;
He leads me beside the still waters.

PSALM 23:1-2 NKJV

❧

A mother's job, of course, is to take care of her children. So we spend most of our time as caregivers. It's a rewarding, fulfilling job—but it can also be tiring. Mothers need to be taken care of, too, if we're to continue to give the best of ourselves.

God, the Great Shepherd, is a mother's caregiver. The Great Shepherd takes care of us by giving us direction in our lives. He walks beside us every day, leading and guiding us gently in the way we should go. He provides for us. He gives us what we need spiritually every day, leading us to still waters and soft green pastures to restore our souls.

All the Great Shepherd needs from us is a willingness to follow Him. We only need to trust Him, one step at a time, to take care of us every moment of every day.

❧

Today we can follow God with open and willing hearts.

I look up to the hills,
but where does my help come from?
My help comes from the LORD,
who made heaven and earth.
He will not let you be defeated.
He who guards you never sleeps.

PSALM 121:1-3 NCV

But I am like an olive tree,
thriving in the house of God.
I trust in God's unfailing love
forever and ever.

PSALM 52:8 NLT

God's Hands

The earth and everything on it belong to the LORD.
The world and its people belong to him.

PSALM 24:1 CEV

❧

"*He*'s got the whole world in His hands," the children sing in Sunday school. Straight from the mouths of babes comes this simple truth—that God, the Creator of this beautiful planet and all the stars above, is in control. God is in control of the great universe—and God is in control of our small, but important, lives.

For mothers this truth comes as a great relief. What freedom this  is! Because God's got the whole world in His hands, we can let God do His job and we are free to do our job. We don't have to be in total control all the time—we can relax knowing that our lives and the lives of our children are in God's very capable hands. Since we don't have to be in total control, all mothers have to do is be responsible and do the very best we can— we can leave the rest to God.

❧

We can relax today because God's got
the whole world in His hands.

Yes, the LORD pours down his blessings.
Our land will yield its bountiful crops.

PSALM 85:12 NLT

✤

O LORD, you have been our refuge
throughout every generation.
Before the mountains were born, before you gave
birth to the earth and the world, you were God.
You are God from everlasting to everlasting.

PSALM 90:1-2 GOD'S WORD

God, Our Teacher

Show me your ways, O Lord,
teach me your paths;
guide me in your truth and teach me,
for you are God my Savior,
and my hope is in you all day long.

PSALM 25:4-5 NIV

Mothers teach our children, but we do much more than help them with their homework. Mothers teach what kids can't get out of a textbook or a classroom—mothers teach our children right from wrong, and show them how to love God, themselves, and others. Where do mothers go to get this heartfelt knowledge?

We turn to God and His words in the Bible. We humbly ask God to instruct our hearts in His way and truth. From God and the Bible we learn right from wrong, and we learn how to love God, ourselves, and others. We pass that knowledge on to our children. For when we teach the way of God, we give them a gift more precious than mere book knowledge—we give them the gift of how to live a happy life at peace with God.

God will teach us His way and truth today.

He leads humble people to do what is right,
and he teaches them his way.
Every path of the LORD is one of mercy and truth
for those who cling to his promise
and written instructions.

PSALM 25:9-10 GOD'S WORD

God's House

*O LORD, I love the house in which you dwell,
and the place where your glory abides.*

PSALM 26:8 NRSV

Our homes are so important to us. It's the place where we can be ourselves. It's the place we feel safest, the most relaxed, and happiest. As mothers, we enjoy taking care of our homes. It's where we raise our children. There's no place like home.

We have another home too. God's home is also our home and our children's home. We go to God's house whenever we go to church.

God's home is bigger than any church—God's home is anywhere God lives. God's home is as big as heaven and as small as the most secret, inner room in our hearts. We love the house in which God dwells—whether it's our local church or the depths of our own hearts. We can go home to visit God and enjoy God's glory anytime we like. For God's house is all around us, above us, and deep inside us.

We can be at home with God anytime we like.

One thing I have asked from the LORD, that I shall seek:
That I may dwell in the house of the LORD all the days of my life,
To behold the beauty of the LORD
And to meditate in His temple.

PSALM 27:4 NASB

God's Peace

The LORD is my light and my salvation; whom shall I fear? The LORD is the strength of my life; of whom shall I be afraid?

PSALM 27:1-2 KJV

Family, friends, and media have told mothers how challenging our job is. "Just wait till they're teenagers." "Paying for college takes a lot of sacrifices." "Your life just isn't your own until they graduate." As if we didn't know. So what? We know that motherhood is the toughest job we'll ever love—challenges included.

With God on our side we can do anything. There is nothing and no one to be afraid of. With God in our corner as we raise and love our children, certainly no challenge is too complicated, no obstacle is insurmountable, and no problem is insoluble. God is the strength of our lives and the lives of our children. Sure, being a mother can be a tough job—but it's also an infinitely joyful one when we trust God to work all things for good.

God is our light and our salvation.
With God all things are possible.

I will listen to what God the LORD will say;
he promises peace to his people, his saints—
but let them not return to folly.

PSALM 85:8 NIV

He alone is my rock and my savior—my stronghold.
I cannot be severely shaken.

PSALM 62:2 GOD'S WORD

God Is Good

Give thanks to the LORD because he is good.
His love continues forever.

PSALM 136:1 NCV

❧

*I*t's all good. We watch our children grow and learn and love and laugh. We enjoy motherhood with all of its blessings, rewards, and challenges. We wouldn't change places with anyone else in the world. Being a mother is all good.

The source of all goodness, of course, is God, and God can't wait to pour His goodness on us—every moment of every day. We don't have to wait to get to heaven to experience how good God is. Every day we pick up the kids at school, help them with their homework, or watch them play in the backyard, we enjoy the goodness of God. Every time we wipe away a tear, hold a little hand to cross the street, or wave good-bye as they go off to summer camp, we touch God's goodness.

We are mothers. We are blessed. For we have seen the goodness of the Lord in the land of the living.

❧

*W*e believe that we shall see the goodness of the Lord today.

Our LORD, everything you do
is kind and thoughtful,
and you are near to everyone
whose prayers are sincere.

PSALM 145:17-18 CEV

I will praise you forever for what you have done;
in your name I will hope, for your name is good.
I will praise you in the presence of your saints.

PSALM 52:9 NIV

The Power of Thanks

*Sing praises to the LORD, O you his faithful ones,
and give thanks to his holy name.*

PSALM 30:4 NRSV

❧

"Thanks, Mom," she says after you've talked with her late into the night about her first prom. "Thanks, Mom," he says, hugging you, his college diploma gripped in his right hand. We don't do it for the thanks, of course. We do it out of love. We'd give them the whole world, if we could, for love alone, but hearing a thank-you is awfully nice. Like icing on a cake.

Imagine how God feels when we give God a thank-You. Our thanks go right to God's heart. It's not just the big things in life we're grateful for. The smaller the blessing, the more powerful our thanks to God who blesses us. We take nothing in our world for granted, for all good gifts come from God. God doesn't do it for the thanks, of course. He does it out of love, but oh how He loves to hear His children give Him a thank-You.

❧

Today we give a thank-You to God
for our world and all that is in it.

Be thankful and praise the LORD
as you enter his temple.

PSALM 100:4 CEV

❧

Let everyone give thanks to you, O God.
Let everyone give thanks to you.

PSALM 67:3 GOD'S WORD

In God's Hand

Into your hands I commit my spirit;
redeem me, O LORD, the God of truth.

PSALM 31:5 NIV

❧

*J*ust getting out the door any weekday morning can be a challenge. Get the kids up and dressed. Make lunches. Take them to school. Then it's off to work and another busy day. With all

that moms have to do in the morning, it's easy to forget God.

As we herd everybody out the door for another day of school and work, we can pray a simple prayer to help us remember who's really driving this bus: "Into Your hands I commit my spirit."

It says to God that You, O Lord, are in control of my life—not me. It says to God, I want to be with You every moment of every day no matter how crazy today gets. It says to God, no matter what happens today, You bring goodness to all who love You. It says to God, I love You. Is there any better way for busy moms to begin the day?

❧

O God, hear this simple prayer—
Into Your hands I commit my spirit.

I follow close behind you;
your strong right hand holds me securely.

PSALM 63:8 NLT

Through Thy righteousness, deliver me and set me free;
incline Thine ear to me and save me.

PSALM 71:2 MLB

The Joy of Forgiveness

Count yourself lucky, how happy you must be —
you get a fresh start,
your slate's wiped clean.

<small>PSALM 32:1 THE MESSAGE</small>

⁊~

Sometimes we make mistakes. Sometimes we act without thinking. Sometimes we don't do our best, but our hearts are in the right place. Our intentions are full of love.

Thank God we moms can go to God for forgiveness! Forgiveness springs from deep love. When we ask God's forgiveness, God looks deep into our hearts and sees the love we have there— and God forgives us. The joy of forgiveness is the ability to start over again. The joy of forgiveness is to love deeper and better than before. The joy of forgiveness is being able to forgive our children and families as God has forgiven us. The joy of forgiveness is freedom from being stuck in the past so we can love again.

The joy of God's forgiveness is available to us anytime, day or night. Our God waits for us with open, loving arms for us to experience the joy of forgiveness.

⁊~

We can ask God's forgiveness anytime we need to.

I come to you, LORD, for protection.
Don't let me be ashamed.
Do as you have promised and rescue me.

PSALM 31:1 CEV

As far as the east is from the west—
that is how far he has removed our rebellious acts from
himself.

PSALM 103:12 GOD'S WORD

A Mother's Blessing

I bless GOD every chance I get;
my lungs expand with his praise.
I live and breathe GOD;
if things aren't going well, hear this and be happy:
Join me in spreading the news;
together let's get the word out.

PSALM 34:1-3 THE MESSAGE

All of us have experienced God's blessings. Of all the blessings of this life, none is greater than our children. Our children are God's living, breathing, and walking blessings. Our children are God's love for us clothed in flesh and blood.

Yes, God has greatly blessed us, but what is it to bless God? What could God possibly want or need from us? God wants us to love Him. We show our love for God every time we praise and bless Him. Our blessings and praise of God put legs on our love for God—our words run straight to God's ears and into God's heart. Blessing God goes beyond thanking God—blessing God is telling God of our wild and boundless love for Him. Because we mothers are mothers, and are deeply, profoundly blessed by God with our children, we naturally return God's blessing by singing God's praises with our lips, with our hearts, with our very lives.

We will bless the Lord all day long; His praise
will always be in our mouths.

We will celebrate and
praise you, LORD!
You are good to us,
and your love never fails.

PSALM 106:1 CEV

God's Faithfulness

God's love is meteoric,
his loyalty astronomic,
His purpose titanic,
his verdicts oceanic.

PSALM 36:5 THE MESSAGE

Mothers know that God's greatest gift is faithfulness. We know that no matter what our children do (or don't do), we will never leave or abandon them. Because we are mothers, we stand with and by our children come what may. Even when our children grow up and have families of their own, our spirits, and our love, never, ever leave them. In other words, mothers are faithful to their children throughout their lives.

No matter what we do (or don't do) in our lives, God will never leave us. God is always, always faithful. God walks with us when times are good; God sustains us when times are tough. God holds each of us in the palm of His hand regardless of how good we are. God's love for us is so deep and wide that God journeys beside us, holding our hand, leading the way through thick and thin. God loves us fiercely with a mother's kind of love. God's faithfulness will never let us go.

God's faithfulness toward us is as vast
as the heavens and as deep as the sea.

How excellent is thy lovingkindness, O God! therefore the
children of men put their trust under the shadow of thy wings.

PSALM 36:7 KJV

Let them give thanks to the LORD for his unfailing love
and his wonderful deeds for men,
for he satisfies the thirsty
and feeds the hungry with good things.

PSALM 107:8-9 NIV

Teach Your Children

I have been young, and now am old;
Yet I have not seen the righteous forsaken,
Nor his descendants begging bread.
He is ever merciful, and lends;
And his descendants are blessed.

PSALM 37:25-26 NKJV

Mothers are naturally generous people. We're very good at giving. One of the most precious gifts a mother can give her child is a generous and open spirit. With a generous spirit a child develops into a secure and confident adult who is able to give out of strength and love. People who learn generosity as children are blessings to their parents.

God wants us to teach our children about generosity. God assures us that when we give liberally, our children become blessings. God returns generosity to us a hundredfold as our children put into practice what they learn from us—to give of themselves, their resources, their love, and their time unconditionally and without fear. We watch our children grow into generous spirits who will one day teach their children the beauty, the quiet spiritual reward of generosity.

God wants us to teach our children to give generously today.

Why should I fear in times of trouble,
when the iniquity of my persecutors surrounds me?

PSALM 49:5 NRSV

❧

I will instruct you and train you
in the way you shall go;
I will counsel you with My eye on you.

PSALM 32:8 MLB

Waiting for God

Rest in the LORD and wait patiently for Him;
Do not fret because of him who prospers in his way,
Because of the man who carries out wicked schemes.

PSALM 37:7 NASB

Mothers know a lot about patience. Our children teach us. We must be patient when our children are learning how to do things for themselves, whether it's learning to tie their shoes or finishing a complicated set of math problems on a school night. We want them to hurry up—there's so much else to do! Patience tells us that we've got to let them learn at their own speed, if they are to learn well.

There's another kind of patience mothers know about too. God teaches us. There are no hard and fast rules to being a good mother. God wants us to learn as we go at our own speed. Sometimes we'd like to be like other moms in the neighborhood, who seem to have it all together, but God isn't finished with us yet. We must patiently wait for God to help us become good moms day by day.

Have patience. God isn't finished with us yet.

Be strong, all who wait with hope for the LORD,
and let your heart be courageous.

PSALM 31:24 GOD'S WORD

Let your blessings reach me, O LORD.
Save me as you promised.

PSALM 119:41 GOD'S WORD

God's Law in a Mother's Heart

I delight to do your will, O my God;
your law is within my heart.

PSALM 40:8 NRSV

It takes a lot of physical energy to be a mom these days. Just keeping up with our children is a full-time job—except many of us also have full-time jobs working for somebody else. It also takes a lot of spiritual and emotional energy to be a good mother. We give our hearts to our kids every moment of every day.

God renews our hearts, gives us the emotional and spiritual strength we need so we can be there for our children one hundred percent. When we keep God's law, God's Word, in our hearts, we find the energy we need for motherhood. Reading the Bible and remembering favorite verses is a tremendous spiritual boost in the midst of a demanding day filled with kids and work. Keeping and meditating on God's law in our hearts gives us a tranquil spirit—a spirit that can help us manage anything.

We have the energy we need for today
because we keep God's law in our hearts.

The law of the LORD is perfect,
converting the soul: the testimony of the LORD
is sure, making wise the simple.

PSALM 19:7 KJV

He counts the stars
and names each one.
Our Lord is great and very powerful.
There is no limit to what he knows.

PSALM 147:4-5 NCV

Praise Worthy

*Then let me go to the altar of God, to God my highest joy,
and I will give thanks to you on the lyre, O God, my God.*

PSALM 43:4 GOD'S WORD

Mother's Day is fun. A lot of what mothers do is taken for granted by our children, but on Mother's Day we become worthy of praise! We're showered with gifts; we're taken out to brunch or dinner. Our churches recognize and honor mothers on Mother's Day. It's a kick!

It's easy sometimes to take all God does for us for granted. The Bible tells us that God, too, is worthy of praise. The next time we have a little time for ourselves, we might try this—proclaim God's Day! Sing God's praises or play music on the stereo that's pleasing to God. Bring gifts of flowers and herbs from the garden inside and dedicate them to God. Make a list of blessings and thank God for each one. Let God's Day be a day of joy, a day of praise, a day of song. Have fun!

Today is God's Day! Today we can sing
and dance and love God!

My praise shall be of thee in the great congregation:
I will pay my vows before them that fear him.

Psalm 22:25 KJV

The Lord reigns, let the earth be glad;
let the distant shores rejoice.

Psalm 97:1 NIV

Simple Joy

O clap your hands, all peoples;
Shout to God with the voice of joy.

PSALM 47:1 NASB

❧

Think for a minute about the simple joys of motherhood. Baby pulls herself up using the sofa and takes her first steps across the  carpet. She floats elegantly down the staircase in her first prom dress. Gravely and proudly, she accepts her college diploma from the dean. Looking tired, but blissful, in a hospital room she adjusts the blanket that holds her own baby— the first grandchild. Nothing—no other experience, no amount of money—can compare to the simple joys our children bring us.

For nurturing and watching our children grow up, we are truly thankful—and we are full of praise to our Creator, who makes all of these moments of joy possible. We want to clap our hands! We want to shout for joy! God, looking down from heaven on our simple joy, rejoices with us—He claps and sings and shouts and all the angels in heaven join in joy.

❧

Clap and shout for joy! God touches our lives!

Great is the LORD and greatly to be praised
in the city of our God.
His holy mountain, beautiful in elevation,
is the joy of all the earth,
Mount Zion, in the far north, the city of the great King.

PSALM 48:1-2 NRSV

Mothers Know

My mouth shall speak wisdom,
And the meditation of my heart shall give understanding.

PSALM 49:3 NKJV

❧

It's common for many new, first-time mothers to fear that they won't know what do or how to care for their babies when they're born. Prior to birth, a lot of soon-to-be new mothers spend anxious months reading up on baby care and parenting. They grill friends with children about what to do; they tell their own mothers that maybe they're not quite ready for motherhood. One day motherhood comes. As the new baby nestles quietly in his mama's arms after birth, a "mother's instinct" kicks in, along with joy, and the new mother just knows it's all going to be all right.

So it is in the life of faith. We don't need to know all the answers beforehand. We need only meditate in our hearts on the love of God day by day. God will give us the understanding, the knowledge we need to journey with Him. The understanding that God gives is like a mother's instinct—we'll know what to do; and it'll be all right.

❧

As we meditate on God's love in our hearts,
we'll know what God wants from us.

I will cry to the God of heaven
who does such wonders for me.

PSALM 57:2 TLB

I remember my song in the night
and reflect on it.

PSALM 77:6 GOD'S WORD

Trusting God

Nevertheless I am continually with you;
you hold my right hand.

PSALM 73:23 NRSV

We've all held the hand of our small children while crossing a busy street. Hand firmly in ours, the child carefully steps off the curb and follows at our side. The child is oblivious to the traffic, content to go where we lead, completely trusting without a thought or understanding of the danger involved in crossing any street.

God desires that same kind of trust from us. God promises to hold our hand no matter what. With our hand firmly in His, God asks that we trust Him, that we follow Him no matter where He leads us. We don't worry or fret or whine. We know God's right hand holds our small, frail human hand. We follow at His side without a care in the world, knowing only that God's love has hold of us and our children.

We can walk confidently through the day
because God holds our hands.

I will sing of the LORD's great love forever;
with my mouth I will make your faithfulness
known through all generations.
I will declare that your love stands firm forever,
that you established your faithfulness in heaven itself.

PSALM 89:1-2 NIV

The LORD looks at the world
from his throne in heaven, and he watches us all.

PSALM 33:13 CEV

Mother's Day

I will remember the deeds of the LORD;
yes, I will remember your miracles of long ago.

PSALM 77:11 NIV

❧

For those of us who've been mothers for many years, Mother's Day is a time for memories. We'll sit at our Mother's Day brunch or dinner and someone will say, "Do you remember when . . . ?"

It's a time when our children tell us what they remember best about their childhood. It's a time when we tell our children funny stories about their growing up years. Our children thank us—and we thank God for our children.

The life of faith is also a time of memories. Of remembering and telling each other stories of what God has done for us. Remembering the deeds of the LORD naturally leads us to thanking God for all we have—especially these precious children, now grown, making memories and stories with their own children. We remember God's wonders of old—and are grateful.

❧

Today we can remember what God has done
for us—and we are thankful.

I will think about each one of your mighty deeds.

PSALM 77:12 CEV

☙

Children are a gift from the LORD; they are a reward from him.

PSALM 127:3 NLT

God's Purpose for Us

We are your people, the sheep of your flock.
We will thank you always;
forever and ever we will praise you.

PSALM 79:13 NCV

❧

*G*od's ways are mysterious, but we know something about His purpose for us in this world. We know God loves us. Because God loves us, God wants us to make sure that generations who come after us love God, recount God's praise, and walk uprightly and in honor on the Earth.

That's where mothers come in. We are part of God's divine purpose to make sure that generation follows generation to give God thanks and praise. The most important part of motherhood is to train and teach and raise our children to love God, to give God thanks and praise, and to grow into honorable adulthood, respecting others and doing good for those less fortunate. What a powerful purpose! Being a mother is a holy calling from God. We are both proud and humbled to carry out God's purpose.

❧

*W*e are mothers. Today we carry out God's purpose for us.

For GOD is great,
and worth a thousand Hallelujahs.
His terrible beauty
makes the gods look cheap;
Pagan gods are mere tatters and rags.
GOD made the heavens—
Royal splendor radiates from him,
A powerful beauty sets him apart.

PSALM 96:3-4 THE MESSAGE

In order that the succeeding
generation might know,
that the children still to be born
might arise and recount it to their sons,
so as to put their confidence in
God and not forget God's works,
but to keep His commandments.

PSALM 78:6-7 MLB

A Mother's Place

Even the sparrow has found a home,
and the swallow a nest for herself,
where she may have her young —
a place near your altar,
O LORD Almighty, my King and my God.

PSALM 84:3 NIV

Maybe it's because we are moms that we love our homes so much. We work to make our homes comfortable, clean places for our families. We browse women's magazines looking for decorating ideas; we try out the latest cleaning products; we install appliances to help us keep our homes neat and tidy; some of us put in long hours in the garden to add to the beauty of our homes. There is truly no place like home. So we spend a lot of time—and money—making sure our homes are the best places they can be.

Home is also a sanctuary. It is where we dwell with God every day. It may not be a very quiet place, filled with children and pets and all. It is a place of peace, a place of wholeness—a place where we and our families can retreat from a fragmented and demanding world to find God.

We are mothers, keepers of God's sanctuary, our homes.

How blessed are those who dwell in Your house!
They are ever praising You.

PSALM 84:4 NASB

Because you have made the LORD, who is my refuge,
Even the Most High, your dwelling place,
No evil shall befall you,
Nor shall any plague come near your dwelling.

PSALM 91:9-10 NKJV

The Power of Self-Control

The LORD God is a sun and shield;
the LORD bestows favor and honor;
no good thing does he withhold
from those whose walk is blameless.

PSALM 84:11 NIV

*R*aising children usually means exercising some self-control

over our lifestyles. Remember what it was like before the children started arriving? Vacations at grown-up destinations instead of theme parks; driving a sporty two-door instead of a minivan; or going to a restaurant with cloth napkins instead of to a fast-food counter that packages happy toys with the meals.

Self-control for the sake of our children is more than lifestyle choices. It's making sure that we live a life that is pleasing to God. Such self-control is not hard—for God gives good things to those who walk uprightly. The benefit to our children is immense—they learn to live like mom, who is generous, grateful, and full of love for God and His ways.

*T*he power of self-control is the love of God. He gives all good things to those who live life with honor and integrity.

Let thy work appear unto thy servants, and thy glory unto their children. And let the beauty of the Lord our God be upon us: and establish thou the work of our hands upon us; yea, the work of our hands establish thou it.

Psalm 90:16-17 kjv

Compassionate Motherhood

Make glad the soul of Your servant,
For to You, O LORD, I lift up my soul.
For You, LORD, are good, and ready to forgive,
And abundant in lovingkindness to all who call upon You.

PSALM 86:4-5 NASB

Mothers are compassionate by nature. One of the things all moms do is cheer up a child who has had a bad day or is

frightened or otherwise sad. We wipe away the tears, and try to divert their attention by helping them to do something happy—maybe a tea party in the backyard or a bike ride around the block or building a fort using a blanket thrown over the dining table.

Our God is compassionate too. Whenever we've had a bad day or are frightened or otherwise sad, we can go to God and ask Him to gladden our hearts. For we know that God is loving and good and forgiving—and God can't wait to help us into happier times. When we come to God like a child who needs cheering up, God will have compassion on us—and we know His goodness and His love will make us happy again.

God will gladden our souls and restore us to happiness again.

Mercy and truth have met together;
Righteousness and peace have kissed.
Truth shall spring out of the earth,
And righteousness shall look down from heaven.

PSALM 85:10-11 NKJV

My lips will praise you
because your mercy is better than life itself.

PSALM 63:3 GOD'S WORD

Gratitude—A Way of Life

I will praise You, O Lord my God, with all my heart,
And I will glorify Your name forevermore.

PSALM 86:12 NKJV

We teach our children to say "please" and "thank you." In a small way it's a way of life. Because saying "please" and "thank you" is more than just being polite—it's what makes us civilized. Saying "please" and "thank you" puts a little oil on the cogs and gears that make day-to-day social life possible. It enormously helps us all to get along together.

Saying "thank You" to God is a way of life. In fact, a life lived in gratitude to God is a life lived in faith. Saying "thank You" to God for His blessings, for watching over us and our children, for His love, mercy, and grace keeps our relationship with God growing. It's more than just being polite. Being grateful to God keeps us from taking God and His work in our lives for granted. Saying "Thank You, God" tells God we want Him in our lives.

We give thanks to God today with our whole hearts.

It is good to give thanks to the LORD,
to sing praises to your name, O Most High;
to declare your steadfast love in the morning,
and your faithfulness by night.

PSALM 92:1-2 NRSV

They eat the rich food in your house,
and you let them drink from your river of pleasure.
You are the giver of life.
Your light lets us enjoy life.

PSALM 36:8-9 NCV

Promise Keeping

Praise the LORD, you his angels,
you mighty ones who do his bidding,
who obey his word.

PSALM 103:20 NIV

Every mother knows how important promises are to children. When children make promises to each other, their promises are sealed with childhood vows to keep them, including chants to "stick a needle in my eye" or spit and handshakes. A child's world stands or falls depending on how well promises are kept. A broken promise brings big tears and wailing condemnation—"but he promised!!"

Mothers are promise keepers. We promise God to keep His words—to love and respect one another, to show mercy and forgiveness, to be women of faith. We promise our children to be the best mothers we can be, to love them and take care of them and raise them well. Our children watch us keeping our promise to God, and they grow up to be promise keepers too. They become people of faith, who love and respect one another, and promise to keep God's words.

We will tell of God's faithfulness and
promise to keep God's words.

You are my inheritance, O Lord.
I promised to hold on to your words.

Psalm 119:57 god's word

⸈

Your word is a lamp for my feet
and a light for my path.

Psalm 119:105 nlt

Guardian Angels

He will command his angels concerning you
to guard you in all your ways.

PSALM 91:11 NRSV

What mother hasn't stood at the front door waving good-bye to her children and said a silent prayer to God? When our children leave us, even for just a little while, we pray for God's angels to defend and protect them. Our children's angels hover over them and journey with them and bring them safely home.

Mothers have guardian angels too. Because we are mothers, and our work is important to God, He sends His angels to guard us in all our ways. We know that when we've had a particularly tough day with the kids or we need extra energy to help them do their homework, our guardian angel hovers over us, whispering encouragement and God's love to our hearts. So the next time we stand at the front door waving good-bye, we know our own guardian angels watch over us and wait with us until our children return safely home.

Today God sends His guardian angels to take care of our children and us.

Because he has set his love upon Me, therefore I will deliver him;
I will set him on high, because he has known My name.
He shall call upon Me, and I will answer him;
I will be with him in trouble;
I will deliver him and honor him.
With long life I will satisfy him,
And show him My salvation.

PSALM 91:14-16 NKJV

Mothers Are Optimists

You, O LORD, have made me glad by what You have done,
I will sing for joy at the works of Your hands.

PSALM 92:4 NASB

❧

*M*others are natural optimists. We look down at the child in our arms and sometimes think, *Maybe he's a future president of the United States, or maybe she'll be a nuclear physicist, or maybe she'll follow in her father's footsteps.* Our dreams for our children make us optimists. That optimism helps give us the energy and foresight we need to make sure that our children's future is bright. We are full of hope.

We are made glad by the works of God's hands, our children. As we hold God's work in our arms, we see a bundle full of promise. Our gladness, our hope is so great it feels as though our souls could burst with joy. Being filled with hope and promise such as this, who can keep from singing praises to God?

❧

*W*e've only to look in our children's eyes to see
that today is filled with hope and promise.

Blessed are all who fear the LORD,
who walk in his ways.

PSALM 128:1 NIV

❧

Our LORD and our God,
you give these blessings to all who worship you.

PSALM 144:15 CEV

The Beauty of Worship

O come, let us worship and bow down: let us kneel before the
LORD our maker. For he is our God; and we are the people
of his pasture, and the sheep of his hand.

PSALM 95:6-7 KJV

❧

*M*others are lots of good things—we're loving, we're resourceful, we're optimistic, we're devoted to our children. There is one thing we're not—we're not in control. We're especially not in control of our children. What a beautiful thing that is. God alone is in control of our lives and the lives of our children and our world. God, our Maker, holds all of us in the palm of His hand. It is God, and God alone, who works for good in our lives.

When we worship God, we acknowledge that we are not in control, and that we have faith and trust that God is in control of our world. What freedom it is to give up trying to be in charge when we don't have to be! What freedom it is to give God the reins and let God do His work! When we worship God, we give up control and we are free to be good mothers and love our children.

❧

*W*e are not shepherds. We are sheep of God's hand.

I bow before your holy Temple as I worship.
I will give thanks to your name
for your unfailing love and faithfulness,
because your promises are backed
by all the honor of your name.
When I pray, you answer me;
you encourage me by giving me
the strength I need.

PSALM 138:2-3 NLT

The Creativity of Motherhood

Sing to the LORD a new song;
sing to the LORD, all the earth.
Sing to the LORD, praise his name;
proclaim his salvation day after day.

PSALM 96:1-2 NIV

Mothers are creative people. We use our creativity to entertain our children on a rainy day—from finger-painting to modeling with clay. We spend hours at the sewing machine to make fun, attractive clothes; we make countless batches of chocolate-chip cookies—all because we love our children. In fact, you could say that motherhood is one big creative project.

In God's hands, mothers are instruments of God's creativity. We are like musical instruments played by a fine musician, who plays songs that are fresh and new and have never been heard before. Through mothers God creates, He brings something new and unique into the world—a child. Children are like new songs—no two, not even twins, are exactly alike. Each child is a new, distinct, irreplaceable person. Each child is a new song that God sings.

Sing to the Lord a new song, for we are instruments in His hands.

You alone created my inner being.
You knitted me together inside my mother.
I will give thanks to you
because I have been so amazingly
and miraculously made.
Your works are miraculous,
and my soul is fully aware of this.

PSALM 139:13-14 GOD'S WORD

Families Tell God's Glory

Ascribe to the LORD, O families of the peoples,
Ascribe to the LORD glory and strength.

PSALM 96:7 NASB

ᖺamilies are a mother's crown and a mother's glory. Not only do we love them deeply, but we're so proud of who they are and what they do in the world. Even the family pet is a special source of pride and joy. Our families tell the world a lot about us as mothers—they make us look good.

Families also tell the world a lot about God. A family bound together by the love and grace of God tells the world that God is loving and merciful. A family who loves and respects each other because of God tells the world that God is strong and good. Not only are our families our own crown and glory, they are the glory of God. Families are God's pride and joy. For through families, God tells the world that He is busy at work in the world.

Our families glorify God; they are jewels in God's crown.

Behold, how good and how pleasant it is for brethren to dwell together in unity!

PSALM 133:1 KJV

Bless the LORD, O house of Israel!
Bless the LORD, O house of Aaron!
Bless the LORD, O house of Levi!
You who fear the LORD, bless the LORD!

PSALM 135:19-20 NKJV

A Quiet Morning with God

*Light dawns for the righteous,
and joy for the upright in heart.*

PSALM 97:11 NRSV

❧

Sometimes we awake early in the morning well before the alarm goes off. The house is so quiet. Time to get ready for school and work is still a ways off. Wide awake, we're faced with a choice—we can toss and turn and fret when sleep won't come, or we can get up and do something useful until sleepiness returns.

Grab a light blanket and a Bible and head for the couch. There in the predawn quiet we can do something truly useful— we can spend a quiet morning with God. We can open the Bible anywhere and read until a verse touches our hearts. We can reread favorite passages and pray. Sometimes, even at three A.M., our hearts may be full of joy—we can even sing quietly to our God, who is the Source of all joy. When sleep finally begins to return, we can thank God for being His child, and tiptoe softly back to bed.

❧

Joy comes in the morning for God's children.

I could say, "The darkness will hide me.
Let the light around me turn into night."
But even the darkness is not dark to you.
The night is as light as the day;
darkness and light are the same to you.

Psalm 139:11-12 NCV

We Know Who We Are

O LORD, You have searched me and known me.

PSALM 139:1 NKJV

What mother hasn't looked at her sleeping child at some time and felt awed and humbled? During such moments we know that this is what life is really all about. We want nothing more than this—than to be the mother of this precious gift, this child.

Humility is a spiritual gift. It doesn't mean we walk around putting ourselves down or thinking badly of ourselves. Instead, true humility is knowing who we really are—and thanking God for who we are in this life. Our friends or the people at work may think they know us, but we know who we really are underneath all those other roles—we are mothers, chosen by God to bring our children life and raise them to love and honor God. Motherhood is a calling that inspires awe—and true humility—in our hearts. We can rejoice and thank God that we know who we are.

Motherhood is a humble, beautiful gift of God.

You know the LORD is God!
He created us, and we belong to him;
we are his people, the sheep in his pasture.

PSALM 100:3 CEV

As a father has compassion on his children,
so the LORD has compassion on those who fear him;
for he knows how we are formed,
he remembers that we are dust.

PSALM 103:13-14 NIV

Mothers Model Integrity

I will sing of lovingkindness and justice,
To You, O LORD, I will sing praises.

PSALM 101:1 NASB

❧

When we're dealing with a person of integrity, we know that "what you see is what you get." A person of integrity does what she says she's going to do. A person of integrity has no hidden agendas. A person of integrity lives her beliefs. A person of integrity inspires trust and loyalty in others. A person of integrity is just a good person.

All mothers want their children to grow up into people of integrity. As mothers we model integrity for our children when our behavior is consistent with our faith—when we keep our promises; when we have mercy on those less fortunate; when we generously share our love of God. In other words, mothers who model integrity "walk the talk." Our children are watching our every move, eager to copy what we do and say. Over the years they grow into strong adults who love God and walk with integrity of heart.

❧

With the love of God and the practice of our faith
let us model integrity for our children.

Your wife will be like a fruitful vine
within your house;
your children will be like olive shoots
around your table.

PSALM 128:3 NRSV

Our Children's Heritage

The children of Your servants will continue,
And their descendants will be established before You.

PSALM 102:28 NKJV

❧

When a mother becomes a grandmother, it's as though all of our dreams have finally come true. It's a different kind of miracle than being a mother. To hold our grandchildren in our arms is to hold a little bit of the future that we will never see. When we're with our grandchildren, we feel ourselves to be a link in an incredibly long and wonderful family chain. We rejoice and give thanks that God has let us see our children's children.

Our faith is for generations. The trust and belief we have in God are gifts to future generations, who will learn from us the joy of loving God. As grandmothers, we can show our grandchildren God's way. It is our grandchildren who will carry our faith deep into the future for generations to come. In a very real sense, a grandmother's faith is forever.

❧

Our children's heritage, our grandchildren,
are the future in God's hands.

You want me to be completely truthful,
so teach me wisdom.

PSALM 51:6 NCV

Some trust in chariots, and some in horses: but we will
remember the name of the LORD our God.

PSALM 20:7 KJV

The Benefits of Believing

Bless the LORD, O my soul,
and all that is within me,
bless his holy name.
Bless the LORD, O my soul,
and do not forget all his benefits.

PSALM 103:1-2 NRSV

❧

Though they may be easy to forget during a particularly hectic day, there are many benefits to motherhood. We get the unparalleled joy of watching our children grow up. We get to play with them as well as take care of them. We get to enjoy the love of our children when they are little. When they are grown, we get to love and enjoy them as adults.

There are many benefits to believing in God too. We get to experience God's mercy and grace when we make mistakes. We get to feel God's love when we look in on our napping children. We get to thank God for giving us all that we need to live and love. We get to worship God, the Creator of our children—and our children's children. We wouldn't trade motherhood or our life of faith for anything in the world.

❧

We will remember all the benefits of believing in God today.

You make the springs pour water into ravines,
so streams gush down from the mountains.
They provide water for all the animals,
and the wild donkeys quench their thirst.
The birds nest beside the streams
and sing among the branches of the trees.

Psalm 104:10-12 nlt

Mothers and Other Living Things

O LORD, how manifold are Your works!
In wisdom You have made them all.
The earth is full of Your possessions —
This great and wide sea,
In which are innumerable teeming things,
Living things both small and great.

PSALM 104:24-25 NKJV

Cats. Dogs. Hamsters. Several frogs over a period of time. A turtle. Goldfish. Maybe a bunny rabbit. Kids and animals go together. Eventually, we get to take care of pets as well as children. The innocence and helplessness of animals and children speak to us. We can't help but love and take care of both.

There's something about being mothers that forms a special connection between the rest of God's creatures and us. Maybe because we bring children into the world, we also know the love God must have for the animals He makes. The connection is creation. Our instinct to love and care for our children—and even their pets—is rooted in our roles as creators with God to bring our children into the world. We rejoice in all God's creatures, great and small.

God loves all the children and animals—and so do we.

Find rest, O my soul, in God alone;
my hope comes from him.
He alone is my rock and my salvation;
he is my fortress, I will not be shaken.
My salvation and my honor depend on God;
He is my mighty rock, my refuge.

PSALM 62:5-7 NIV

Mothers Don't Give Up

Seek the LORD, and his strength: seek his face evermore. Remember his marvellous works that he hath done; his wonders, and the judgments of his mouth; O ye seed of Abraham his servant, ye children of Jacob his chosen.

PSALM 105:4-6 KJV

*M*others persevere. It's not in our nature to give up when the going gets a little tough. Sure, we've got a lot on our plates—in

addition to being full-time moms, a lot of us have full-time jobs, but we manage. We cope. Most of the time, we juggle our lives very well—we have to because the happiness and well-being of our children are at stake.

Mothers persevere in another way too. We are always seeking God and His strength. There's so much to do that we can't afford not to. We know that when we are in touch with God, God will give us all we need to be good mothers. We know that when we search for God, we find that God is not only looking down on us from heaven but is also right here walking beside us.

*T*oday we can persevere because we have found God.

The LORD is my strength, my shield from every danger.
I trust in him with all my heart.
He helps me, and my heart is filled with joy.
I burst out in songs of thanksgiving.

PSALM 28:7 NLT

Love Is Forever

For great is your love, higher than the heavens;
your faithfulness reaches to the skies.

PSALM 108:4 NIV

❧

*A*mother's love is limitless. Our love for our children doesn't stop when they grow up. Instead our love deepens and grows with them. When our children have children of their own, even more love is born in our hearts. A mother's love is so big it even expands beyond our own families to include friends and neighbors. When we became mothers, God gave us very big hearts.

God's love is forever. God loves us and our children and all that is in our world, His creation. God's love is not limited by time. God pours His love on us all of our days—and well beyond, in heaven. There is no place we can go that God's love can't find us. There is nothing we can do to stop God from loving us. Touched by God's forever love as we are, we know that our hearts are so full of faith, it's hard to keep from singing.

❧

*O*ur love is limitless because God loves us forever.

I'm ready, God, so ready,
ready from head to toe.
Ready to sing,
ready to raise a God-song:
"Wake, soul! Wake, lute!
Wake up, you sleepyhead sun!"

PSALM 108:1-3 THE MESSAGE

He ransoms me from death
and surrounds me with love and tender mercies.

PSALM 103:4 NLT

A Mother's Comfort

It was you who took me from the womb;
you kept me safe on my mother's breast.
On you I was cast from my birth,
and since my mother bore me you have been my God.

PSALM 22:9-10 NRSV

A mother's life is filled with adventure. The adventure begins when our children come into our life. Along the way we love them. We nurse them when they are sick. We help them with their schoolwork. We coach them through Little League, ballet, soccer, or violin lessons. We clean up after them and nag them about finishing everything on their plates. Through all the adventures motherhood brings, God travels with us and watches over us and comforts us.

Suddenly our children graduate, marry, and have children of their own. Our love swells with pride. We know they have begun a great adventure. Even though we may shed tears of joy and pride as our children set off on their journeys, we know that God goes with them—to love them as God has loved them from birth—and a mother's heart is comforted.

At the beginning of all great adventures in life, we can take comfort in how our God loves us with a mother's love.

When I am afraid, I put my trust in you.
O God, I praise your word.
I trust in God, so why should I be afraid?
What can mere mortals do to me?

Psalm 56:3-4 NLT

The Apple of God's Eye

Guard me as the apple of the eye;
hide me in the shadow of your wings.

PSALM 17:8 NRSV

Motherhood is all about giving. We give our time and love in abundance to raise our children well. We give because our children are the apples of our eyes. How could we possibly give anything less than our whole selves?

To keep giving every minute of every day, mothers need lots of strength. Knowing how much God loves us is the strength that can keep us going. God loves each one of us deeply and faithfully because each of us is the apple of God's eye, protected under the shadow of God's wing. We are so dear to God; God loves us as His children. God gives us what we need every day so we can give even more to the apples of our eyes. Under the shadow of God's wing, we draw strength from which we give.

You are a mother—the apple of God's eye, kept safe under the shadow of God's wing.

I go to bed and sleep in peace,
because, LORD, only you keep me safe.

PSALM 4:8 NCV

As the mountains surround Jerusalem,
so the LORD surrounds his people
both now and forevermore.

PSALM 125:2 NIV

Time for God

As a deer longs for flowing streams,
so my soul longs for you, O God.
My soul thirsts for God,
for the living God.

PSALM 42:1-2 NRSV

Mothers are very busy people. There are carpools to drive. Scraped knees to bandage. Meals to cook. Homework to oversee. A lot is crammed into a mother's day—usually at the beginning and the end of a busy day at the office.

To keep going—and loving—at such a fast clip, we need to replenish our own thirsty souls. We need time with God, even if it's only a stolen moment or two on the run. Simply thinking about God, who loves us deeply, can quench our thirst for a while. Or thanking God for the love of children and home can keep us going when we're dashing off to the next thing. If a mother's faith is to stay strong, a drink from the heavenly fountain can sustain and nurture us in all we do.

Today may be busy, but we can take a moment to drink from God's flowing streams.

Deal bountifully with Your servant,
That I may live and keep Your word.
Open my eyes, that I may behold
Wonderful things from Your law.

PSALM 119:17-18 NASB

If you have enjoyed this book, you will also enjoy other gift books available from your local bookstore.

GIFTS FROM MY GARDEN
GIFTS FROM MY FRONT PORCH
DAILY BLESSINGS FOR MY HUSBAND
DAILY BLESSINGS FOR MY WIFE
DAILY BLESSINGS FOR MY SECRET PAL
LETTERS FROM GOD
LETTERS FROM GOD FOR TEENS
FRIENDSHIP PSALMS
LIGHTHOUSE PSALMS
GARDEN PSALMS
LOVE PSALMS
PSALMS FOR FATHERS
PSALMS FOR WOMEN

*If this book has impacted your life,
we would like to hear from you.*

Please contact us at:

*Honor Books
Department E
P. O. Box 55388
Tulsa, Oklahoma 74155*

*Or by e-mail at:
info@honorbooks.com*